WOMEN
OF THE
WORD

BIBLE
STUDY
SERIES

FROM
SHAME
TO
BEAUTY

MARIE POWERS

Gospel Light

Published by Gospel Light
Ventura, California, U.S.A.
www.gospellight.com
Printed in the U.S.A.

© 2010 Aglow International. All rights reserved.
Previously published in 1998 in the Aglow Bible Study
series as *Shame: Thief of Intimacy*.

Aglow International is an interdenominational organization of
Christian women. Our mission is to lead women to Jesus Christ and provide
opportunity for Christian women to grow in their faith and minister to others.
Our publications are used to help women find a personal relationship with
Jesus Christ, to enhance growth in their Christian experience, and to help them
recognize their roles and relationships according to Scripture. For more
information about our organization, please write to Aglow International,
P.O. Box 1749, Edmonds, WA 98020-1749, U.S.A., or call (425) 775-7282.
For ordering or information about the Aglow studies and other
resources, visit the Aglow E-store at www.aglow.org.

Rights for publishing this book outside the U.S.A. or in non-English languages are
administered by Gospel Light Worldwide, an international not-for-profit ministry.
For additional information, please visit www.glww.org, email info@glww.org, or write
to Gospel Light Worldwide, 1957 Eastman Avenue, Ventura, CA 93003, U.S.A.

To order copies of this book and other Gospel Light products in bulk quantities,
please contact us at 1-800-446-7735.

To my husband, Jim,
whose courage in breaking through his
own walls of shame in order to walk in
relationship has been an example to many,
especially our children.

CONTENTS

OREWORD

One day as Peter and John were about to enter the temple to pray, they came upon a man lame from his mother's womb. He was carried to the temple gate called Beautiful and there asked alms of those who were entering. Seeing Peter and John, of course the man asked for alms. Little did he realize that what he was about to receive was far beyond a few shekels to help sustain his weak, weary body just to get it through one more day.

"Silver and gold I do not have," Peter responded, "but I have something greater, something that will go to the core (source) of your lameness and bring wholeness to your life. In the name of Jesus Christ of Nazareth, rise up and walk." Immediately the lame man received strength (see Acts 3:1-10).

The man wasn't lame because of a recent illness, such as a degenerative disease. Nor was he lame due to an accident that caused him to stumble. He came into the world lame. He was lame from his mother's womb! He entered the world without strength, without the ability to live life in a healthy way. In a sense, he came into the world a beggar. And this is how we have all come into the world.

Because of the fall of man, we all know a certain "crippledness" that hinders us from living life and from walking in the true joy of healthy relationships with God and with others. In this study, Marie identifies a profound form of our crippledness, and brings us through to a place of healing.

Through the pages of this study, you will see yourself again and again. As you read, you will hear the truth of God's Word spoken clearly to your heart, saying, "In the name of Jesus Christ of Nazareth, rise up and walk" (Acts 3:6).

I pray that as surely as the lame man at the Beautiful Gate received strength and wholeness, you, too, will find yourself leaping and praising God for your newfound health and vitality.

Jane Hansen-Hoyt
International President
Aglow International

INTRODUCTION

Two Kinds of Shame

LEGITIMATE SHAME

A major principle in God's master plan is that His people would walk in the light, a foundational condition for true fellowship (see 1 John 1:7). He intends that His people be open, honest, transparent, and free of masks and other self-protective strategies that keep us hidden from one another. Such was the figurative description of Adam and Eve before sin entered the world. They were naked and were not ashamed (see Genesis 2:25).

Then came the Fall.

God's first two humans disobeyed God's specific command. They sinned and knew they were naked. In fear and shame they scrambled to hide themselves. Frantically they sewed fig leaves together to cover themselves from each other. Then they hid from God (see Genesis 3:8).

Thus, the terrible consciousness of shame entered the human soul. As traumatic and awful as it was to experience, their sense of shame caused a good thing. Good because it alerted them to the guilt of their sin and caused them to admit their failure. Good because it opened the door for God to provide a covering for their nakedness—a foreshadowing of Jesus' death for us on the cross—that would be an eternal solution instead of the pitiful efforts of their own hands (see Genesis 3:21).[1]

God's intention for the awful sense of shame was that it would drive us to Him for forgiveness and restoration. This legitimate shame is directly connected to being wrong before God and is designed to be temporary. Once forgiven, we're healed of our shame, and God intends that it be gone.

God's remedy for legitimate shame is the cross of Christ.

FALSE SHAME

There is another kind of shame, however, one that does not originate with God. This kind seems to have no beginning point, appears to have no remedy, and seems inescapable. The feelings of this kind of shame— we'll call it false shame—are the same as those of legitimate shame: fear of being found out, naked and exposed, and fear of humiliation, rejection and ultimately abandonment. And we have the same need to hide our-selves from others.

The difference is that these feelings are not connected with sinful things we have done but with how we perceive ourselves at the core of our being: somehow flawed, irreparably defective, lacking in whatever we think quali-fies us as fully acceptable members of the human race. As Christians living on the redemption side of the Cross, we should be impervious to such tor-menting thoughts. The truth is, we're not. Many of us continue to struggle with a deep sense of "not quite making it" or "not quite being enough."

Enter Satan, the accuser of the brethren (see Revelation 12:10).

Satan not only accuses us before God day and night, but he also ac-cuses us in our own minds. His goal is to cripple us for God's purposes and rob us of a fully lived life.

The *Spirit-Filled Life Bible* defines Satan as, "An opponent, or the Op-ponent; the hater; the accuser; the adversary; enemy; one who resists, ob-structs, and hinders whatever is good."[2] He hinders us by continually whispering in our ears thoughts of inadequacy, inferiority and comparison with others. He knows the areas that are especially painful to each person and he reminds us of them over and over again.

We think they are our thoughts. Over the years they have become truth to us. To compensate, we wear masks instinctively constructed and put in place long ago to hide our unacceptable selves from the world. These, too, have become part of us and now seem like "who we are."

The reason we call this false shame is because it is built on lies.

The remedy for legitimate shame is the Cross.

The remedy for false shame is the truth.

The goal of this Bible study is to help uncover the lies we've believed and to be set free by God's truth.

If you are not in a group, we encourage you to go through the study with one other person, someone with whom you can discuss what you're learning. Seek someone you can pray with, someone who will keep you ac-countable.

An Overview of the Study

This Bible study is divided into four sections:

1. *A Closer Look at the Problem* defines the problem and the goal of the study.

2. *A Closer Look at God's Truth* gets you into God's Word. What does God have to say about what you are facing? How can you begin to apply His Word as you work through each lesson?

3. *A Closer Look at My Own Heart* will help you clarify and further apply biblical truths in your own life. It will also give guidance as you work toward becoming free from shame.

4. *Action Steps I Can Take Today* is designed to help you focus on immediate steps of action.

WHAT YOU WILL NEED

• *A Bible*—The main Bible version used in this study is the *New King James Version*, but you can use whatever Bible translation you are used to reading.

• *A Notebook*—During this study you will want to keep a journal to record what God shows you personally. You may also want to journal additional thoughts or feelings that come up as you go through the lessons. Some questions may require more space than is given in this study book.

• *Time to Meditate*—Only through meditation on what you're learning will you hear God's Word for you and begin to experience a heart knowledge, as well as a head knowledge, of the subject of being free from shame. Give the Holy Spirit time to personalize His Word to your heart so that you can know what your response should be to the knowledge you are gaining.

Notes
1. God covered Adam and Eve with a covering of His making that required the shedding of blood of innocent animals. That act pointed to Jesus, the innocent sacrifice for our sins.
2. Jack Hayford, General Editor, *Spirit-Filled Life Bible* (Nashville, TN: Thomas Nelson, Inc., 1991), p. 710.

HOW TO START AND LEAD A SMALL GROUP

One key to leading a small group is to ask yourself, *What would Jesus do and how would He do it?* Jesus began His earthly ministry with a small group called the disciples, and the fact of His presence made wherever He was a safe place to be. Think of a small group as a safe place. It is a place that reflects God's heart and His hands. The way in which Jesus lived and worked with His disciples is a basic small-group model that we are able to draw both direction and nurture from.

Paul exhorted us to "walk in love, as Christ also has loved us and given Himself for us" (Ephesians 5:2). We, as His earthly reflections, are privileged to walk in His footsteps, to help bind up the brokenhearted as He did or simply to listen with a compassionate heart. Whether you use this book as a Bible study, or as a focus point for a support group, a church group or a home group, walking in love means that we "bear one another's burdens" (Galatians 6:2). The loving atmosphere provided by a small group can nourish, sustain and lift us up as nothing else can.

Jesus walked in love and spoke from an honest heart. In His endless well of compassion He never misplaced truth. Rather, He surrounded it with mercy. Those who left His presence felt good about themselves because Jesus used truth to point them in the right direction for their lives. When He spoke about the sinful woman who washed Jesus' feet with her tears and wiped them with her hair, He did not deny her sin. He said, "Her sins, which are many, are forgiven, for she loved much" (Luke 7:47). That's honesty without condemnation.

Jesus was a model of servant leadership (see Mark 10:43-44). One of the key skills a group leader possesses is the ability to be an encourager of the group's members to grow spiritually. Keeping in personal contact with each member of the group, especially if one is absent, tells each one that he or she is important to the group. Other skills an effective group leader demonstrates include being a good listener, guiding the discussion, as well as guiding the group to deal with any conflicts that arise within it.

Whether you're a veteran or brand new to small-group leadership, virtually every group you lead will be different in personality and dynamic. The constant is the presence of Jesus Christ, and when He is at the group's center, everything else will come together.

OU'RE INVITED!

TO GROW . . .

*To develop and reach maturity; thrive; to spring up;
come into existence from a source;*

WITH A GROUP . . .

*An assemblage of persons gathered or located together;
a number of individuals considered together because of similarities;*

TO EXPLORE . . .

*To investigate systematically; examine; search into or range over
for the purpose of discovery;*

NEW TOPICS

Subject of discussion or conversation.

MEETING

Date _____ Time _____

Place _____

_____

Contact _____

Phone _____

ONE

CONTRIBUTORS TO SHAME

The following note was given to me by someone who understood the power of shame in her life:

> My earliest memory of school was an older boy who pointed at me and loudly remarked, "You are fat!" His friends took up the chant and I was devastated. I ran home to Mamma and she assured me that he was wrong. I was just the right weight. I didn't believe her.
>
> To this day, regardless of my weight, I feel fat. I wear clothes that disguise my body shape, avoid activities that require special clothing. While on a trip to Hawaii, I refused to wear a bathing suit. I finally went swimming in a pair of baggy below-the-knee shorts.
>
> Even though my husband tells me he likes the way I look, I just can't believe him. I'm ashamed of my appearance.
>
> Another area of shame for me is my teeth. As a child I was always told how pretty and cute I was. I never believed it and was proved right when I overheard a family friend comment how my crooked front teeth spoiled my smile.
>
> From that day on, embarrassed by my crooked teeth, I refused to smile. In family photos I'm usually hiding behind someone or my hand is firmly planted over my mouth. At 25 years of age I had my teeth straightened. Now I'm embarrassed by how yellow they look.

For another example, consider this excerpt from a story that appeared in the *Pacific* magazine section of the *Seattle Times* newspaper about a young man who also struggled mightily with feelings of shame and unacceptance.

Gary sat with the newspaper reporter at the Emerald Cup Body-building Championship, the highlight event of the year for him. "The meat," as Gary called the heavyweight contenders, "came out one by one, a parade of cut-up flesh and veins."

Gary had come to pay homage to the god of muscle, and in words that affirmed his reverance and yearning, he said of the man walking off the stage: "He—was—HUGE."

Gary talked to the reporter about the psychology of Big and Small. He said he had at various times been both. To Gary, to be big was worth risking his health and his family. He began popping and shooting steroids as a high school junior and went from a short and slight 140 pounds to a short and muscled 184. He graduated high school with the honor of "Best Physique." Eventually the steroids caused him to become violent. He was kicked out of his home and lost most of his friends. Still, that didn't stop him; the reward of a powerful body image and the distant admiration of others was worth everything to him for a while.

"When you're big, it's like you have this invisible shield around you," declared Gary. "People clear a path. No one'll mess with you. But they'll look at you. You walk down the street and everybody'll turn their head. You're like a Mercedes Benz driving down the road.

"You feel like you have authority, you feel like God. You're a monster. No one can touch you."

So "being big in body is equated to being big in life," observed the reporter. "When you're scrawny or flabby, you're nothing. Or close to it."

Over the last year, though, it had begun to dawn on Gary that in many ways his quest to become monstrously huge was futile. "Because you never get there. You're never at your ultimate peak. No matter how big you get, you wanna get bigger. So you work even harder, you take more steroids, you pump more weight and pretty soon it's your whole life and you're still not there!"

Shame is a terrible thing. It was never intended to be the portion for God's children. Yet, many of us can deeply relate to the feelings illustrated by the two stories above.

In Scripture, shame is reserved for the enemies of God and those of His people. It is the eternal condition of those who do not come to Christ, "the legacy of fools" Proverbs 3:35 talks about. In the Resurrection, those whose names are not written in the book of life will be raised "to shame and everlasting contempt" (Daniel 12:2).

But God has something better for His people. He wants us to be free from the fear of being uncovered, exposed and found wanting, secure in the knowledge that we are eternally clothed in His righteousness.

In the introduction we discovered that there is a difference between the conviction of sin, which has an immediate solution in Christ, and the nagging, pervasive sense of irreparable defectiveness that seems to have no remedy. Satan, the enemy of our souls, is the author of the latter. We need to become wise to his tactics because the resulting self-protectiveness not only hinders us but also the work of God through us. The goal of this chapter is to uncover some of the main contributors to false shame—hereafter referred to as shame.

A Closer Look at the Problem

Someone said, "Shame develops because of broken interpersonal bridges." This may begin before we are born. Behavioral scientists now believe it is possible that unborn babies can sense the emotions of their mothers. If this is so, we can understand how a baby, even before birth, could begin to develop fears or insecurity. The baby's primary interpersonal bridge could be threatened before his or her first breath.

What are some conditions of pregnancy that you think might threaten a baby's sense of security?

_____

_____

_____

_____

_____

Why?

_____

_____

_____

_____

Shame begins to develop in children before they can put words to their feelings. Naturally narcissistic and very self-relating, they tend to interpret events and others' actions as being about them. Anger in the home and neglect or abuse of any kind become judgments about them. Left to themselves, they are incapable of evaluating adult behavior objectively. They can only evaluate their worth in the light of that behavior. To them, bad things mean they are bad people.

As children get older, another great contributor to shame is any sense of difference from others, especially if others point it out. Stuttering, learning disabilities, body shape and size, or even hair color can contribute to a child's sense of not having what it takes to be acceptable in life. Events such as a death in the family, a divorce, or having a sibling who is challenged by a birth defect or mental disability can be interpreted by a child as a statement about his or her worth.

Among the most crippling of contributors to shame is sexual abuse. This causes extremely deep shame and devastates the child at the very center of his or her being. First Corinthians 6:18 tells us that sexual sin is more violating than other kinds because all other sin is outside the body. The same principle applies to sexual abuse: It violates victims at their core.

Perhaps the most pervasive and powerful source of shameful feelings and the resulting self-rejection in this generation is the media: TV, movies, magazines, videos. Our sensibilities are bombarded on every side by standards for appearance, possessions and position. Advertising is skillfully crafted to hook us at our deepest sense of defectiveness. "The relentless pursuit of perfection" is the appeal of one luxury-car manufacturer.

Children are especially vulnerable to this constant indoctrination. Little girls in primary grades are already aware of their body shapes in today's Barbie™ society. Before they understand how and why their bodies grow, some think they have already missed the mark. Consequently, we hear of dieting among eight- and nine-year-olds. Very possibly, the seeds of eating disorders are already being planted.

Respond to this statement: "Children are terrific observers but terrible interpreters."

_____
_____
_____
_____

_____

_____

_____

A Closer Look at God's Truth

Read the following Bible verses and underline the word "shame" in each one:

> If you confess with your mouth, "Jesus is Lord," and believe in your heart that God raised him from the dead, you will be saved. For it is with your heart that you believe and are justified, and it is with your mouth that you confess and are saved. As the Scripture says, "Anyone who trusts in him will never be put to shame" (Romans 10:9-11, *NIV*).

> "Because you say, 'I am rich, and have become wealthy, and have need of nothing,' and you do not know that you are wretched and miserable and poor and blind and naked, I advise you to buy from Me gold refined by fire, that you may become rich, and white garments, that you may clothe yourself, and that the shame of your nakedness may not be revealed; and eyesalve to anoint your eyes, that you may see" (Revelation 3:17-18, *NASB*).

These verses apply to legitimate shame that is the result of sin. What are we told is the answer to this awful dilemma?

_____

_____

_____

_____

Earlier we talked about false shame and how God never intended for His children to feel vulnerable, unclothed and fearful of rejection. Read Psalm 139:1-18. What do you discover about yourself before you were even born?

_____

_____

_____

_____

As you read the following verses, list the truths that counter the lies you have been fed:

Romans 8:28-39

_____

_____

_____

_____

_____

_____

Philippians 1:6

_____

_____

_____

_____

_____

Hebrews 13:20-21

_____

_____

_____

_____

_____

_____

Make a thoughtful list of personal characteristics or events in your life, beginning with your childhood, that you believe contributed to negative self-judgments.

_____

_____

_____

_____

_____

_____

_____

_____

A Closer Look at My Own Heart

A person's core beliefs about himself or herself are usually in place before adolescence. Most of us go into adulthood with a wounded child's view of who we are. Some of us continue to live out of that perspective, never stopping to reevaluate our belief system. Most often, life's events from there on contribute to and reinforce the shame base that has already been established. Because shame comes into our lives from many sources, it is a mistake to assume that if we come from warm, functional homes we have missed being affected by this toxic emotion.

A good definition of shame is "a painful belief in one's basic defectiveness as a human being."

Action Steps I Can Take Today

Summarize the truth you have discovered today into a brief paragraph. Be sure to include truth from an adult, Christ-centered point of view.

_____

_____

_____

_____

_____

_____

_____

_____

Pray. Ask God to help you make His truth your truth. Ask Him to help you persevere as you continue in your quest for freedom in Christ.

TWO

CHARACTERISTICS OF SHAME

Erin, a tall, pretty strawberry-blond spoke first at the end of my teaching session. "When you introduced your topic tonight, I thought, *Well, this will be good information to have so I can help someone else, but it doesn't apply to me. I don't have a problem with shame.*" Erin paused a moment. "But the more you described it the more I realized—I have a big problem with shame!"

Erin expressed the sentiments of many when they first hear about the subject of shame. After all, they're coping; they don't appear to have any deep emotional problems. It sounds like such an awful thing; it can't apply to "normal" people. But it does. Shame affects all of us to one degree or another. It is precisely because of the apparent normalcy of it that it remains undetected.

Some of us don't know we have a disease until, through some discovery (probably hearing someone else describe their experience), we become aware that certain bothersome problems we've been having are actually characteristics of a specific illness. When we know what it is, we can get the right treatment. Most of us experience the uncomfortable, sometimes excruciating symptoms of shame, but we've had them so long we think they're normal.

Our goal in this chapter is to give us a diagnostic list, not exhaustive by any means, by which we may identify our condition. This is the first step toward healing.

A Closer Look at the Problem

Please keep in mind that every characteristic on the following list may not apply to every person. People suffer from varying degrees of shame. Some are more crippled by it than others, but all are affected to some degree.

STRUGGLE WITH LOW SELF-ESTEEM

A shame base becomes established in our hearts only when we begin to take sides against ourselves and come into agreement with the voices of unacceptability we hear (or think we hear) around us. It's like stepping outside of one's self and saying, "Something really *is* wrong with you. You don't have what other people have. I don't like you, either!" This disowning of one's self probably doesn't happen in a single event, but becomes an attitude over time.

HAVE A PREVAILING LOW-GRADE DEPRESSION

When we have decided we are unacceptable, we cannot help but have an inner sense of depression about ourselves. This condition cannot always be judged from the outside. Some crack jokes and try to keep people laughing. Actually, it's a façade for their own inner sadness. Much depression is caused from a "loss of self." When we reject ourselves we have lost ourselves in the most literal sense of the word.

HAVE A "SHAME GRID"

External events and circumstances tend to indict us. A shame grid is like a filter that sifts all incoming information and gives it a little bit of a twist so that it becomes a negative statement about ourselves. In actuality, we're the person most often indicting ourselves. A compliment about someone else is not heard as a compliment about them; it is heard as an indictment about me. This is especially true if the affirmation is in an area where I get some of my identity—motherhood, homemaking, ministry gifts, appearance, possessions, and so forth When someone is lauded for his or her talents or accomplishments in these areas, in my ears it often becomes a judgment about my inadequacies. Although the statement was not associated with me, my feelings of not being enough, having enough, or doing enough are stirred afresh.

COMPARE AND COMPETE

The acceptability of ourselves as people with shame depends on how we compare with others. We know what the acceptable standards are in weight, shape, beauty, material possessions, career, ministry, how successful our children are or whether or not we're married, and so forth.

Our view of ourselves depends on how we measure up to those standards. Even if we've dropped out of competition, it may not mean we're free of shame; it may only mean we gave up altogether. As a defense, we may become hostile about the standard, even loudly decry it, but inside we're still not free. We're only trying to change the standard so we can compete.

Shame also causes us to focus on what we deem our "unacceptable" parts so that even our successes are made of no account; for example, a student who gets all As feels like a failure because she is overweight.

CAN'T BEAR CRITICISM
Those with shame do not differentiate between who they are and what they've done. Any criticism is heard as an evaluation of themselves as a person. When someone says, "You made a mistake," they hear, "You are a mistake." For them, hearing that something is wrong means they are wrong. That hurts. Often their response is to leave the situation.

BLAME OTHERS FOR MISTAKES
This is related to being unable to bear criticism. Mistakes are interpreted as a personal judgment, so they must find someone else to blame.

FEEL AS IF THEY DON'T BELONG
They feel they're different from others, and others know it just by looking at them. Aware of a certain "correct" standard in the world that one must meet, they feel they never quite make it. Keith Miller expressed his feelings of not belonging when he wrote, "It was as if other people had been given a secret manual about how to get along and be loved and at home in life and I hadn't got one."[1]

EXCRUCIATINGLY SELF-FOCUSED
They can be in a room of 50 and feel like everyone notices and judges them. One very average-sized woman said, "I never get up and walk across the room at social gatherings, because I know everyone will look at me and think how fat I am." Similarly, they feel that every mistake will be remembered forever. They often go home and replay everything they've said all evening.

APPEARANCE-ORIENTED
How things look is what is important, not what is real. They have to look like the perfect Christian family or the perfect Christian couple, even if

they're dying inside. The worst thing is not that they don't have it together, it's that others will *find out* that they don't have it together. Fear of exposure is the driving force behind the creation of façades.

IDOLATROUS
This means that they get their identity from something other than who they are in Jesus: their own performance, things, someone else's performance (husband, wife, child). For some of us, the idol is Christian ministry—getting our worth from what we're doing for God instead of what God has done for us in Christ.

OFTEN BECOME ADDICTED
Self-alienation results in alienation from others. Addiction is an attempt to fill our hunger for real relationship with things or activities, rather than true interaction with people. Food, alcohol, drugs, TV, pornography, reading, work, Christian ministry, helping others (not to be confused with genuinely relating to others), can all be attempts to escape the painful feelings of inner isolation.

WANT INTIMACY, BUT PUSH IT AWAY
When others begin to respond with overtures of intimacy, shame-based people often sabotage the relationship. Intimacy means exposure, and exposure in their minds means pain and humiliation. People deeply affected by shame have spent their whole lives protecting themselves and will not easily let their guard down.

BLACK OR WHITE; ALL OR NOTHING
Either they become perfectionistic or give up altogether. Ordinary is not okay. What they do must be done perfectly to prevent their own flaws from being exposed. Or they do nothing, because "nothing" cannot be criticized.

UNAWARE OR DISHONEST WITH FEELINGS
They become experts at stuffing emotions. Feelings hurt too much and make them vulnerable. A person with shame sees feelings as weaknesses, something to be guarded against. They become experts in talking with *thinking* words, not *feeling* words, for example, "How did you feel when you were fired from your job?" "Well, I didn't think it was very fair. I thought

my boss was a jerk!" As opposed to, "I felt betrayed and hurt. I was scared I wouldn't find another job. I felt like a failure."

TIRED

Self-protection, even if happening unconsciously, is hard work. Working in concert with our efforts to hide our unacceptable, real selves from others is our instinctive drive to construct an acceptable self that we offer to the world. Because all this is the work of our own hands, not the creative energy of God, it drains us.

A Closer Look at God's Truth

How we view ourselves determines our freedom from shame. Low self-esteem is always the result of looking in the wrong place for who we are.

The word "esteem" means "to appraise or assess value." Our self-appraisal or assessment needs to agree with God's appraisal and value of us.

We must confess what God confesses. To confess means to agree with God, to say what God says.

Read Matthew 13:45-46. In our fallen condition, we were spiritually bankrupt and had nothing of value that we could sell. Neither can Jesus be "bought." Paul declares in 1 Corinthians 6:20 and again in 7:23 that you were bought with a price. With these comments in mind, who must the merchant in the parable of Matthew 13:45-46 represent?

_____

_____

_____

_____

_____

_____

Who are the pearls of great value?

_____

_____

_____

_____

_____

_____

What is Jesus saying about us?

_____

_____

_____

_____

_____

_____

Read John 3:16. How does it make you feel to realize that you are so valuable that the very God of the universe gave the life of His most valued possession (His Son, Jesus) to redeem you and buy you back for Himself?

_____

_____

_____

_____

_____

_____

Does your assessment of yourself agree with God's assessment of you? The following Scriptures will help you reassess who you are:

Ephesians 1:4-6

_____

_____

_____

_____

_____

Ephesians 2:4-10

_____

_____

_____

_____

_____

1 John 3:1

_____

_____

_____

_____

_____

A Closer Look at My Own Heart

Accepting ourselves and being honest with others can be risky. Catholic philosopher Roman Guardini states, "The act of self-acceptance is the root of all things. I must agree to be the person whom I am. Agree to have the qualifications I have. Agree to live within the limitations set for me. . . . The clarity and courageousness of this acceptance is the foundation of all existence."[2]

Look back at the characteristics of shame-based people in "A Closer Look at the Problem" (pages 24-27). Reread this list slowly and prayerfully as you ask yourself, "Have I ever felt this way? Can I recall specific incidents when I was aware of these particular feelings?" Writing down your thoughts will help you see more clearly.

Now prayerfully consider and list the parts of yourself you find hard to accept. Ask the Lord for His viewpoint as you meditate on 1 Corinthians 12:12-30. (You may want to use your notebook for this.)

_____

_____

_____

_____

_____

Action Steps I Can Take Today

Ask God to give you the courage to lay before Him the area of your life that you're most concerned with today.

Is there someone with whom you can be accountable concerning this area? Someone who would be committed to pray with you on a regular basis? If there is, call him or her.

Notes

1. Keith Miller's quote from Terry Hershey, *Go Away, Come Closer* (Dallas, TX: Word Publishing, 1990), Introduction, p. x.
2. Walter Trobisch, *Love Yourself* (Downers Grove, IL: InterVarsity Press, 1976), p. 9. Some of the characteristics of shame-based people listed in this lesson were gleaned from a message by Jeff Van Vonderen.

THREE

CAUSE AND COVERS FOR SHAME

PART ONE: CAUSE OF SHAME

In chapter 1, we addressed the development of shame since infancy. In chapter 2, we noted that shame becomes established in our hearts only when we come into agreement with the negative—real or perceived—voices we hear.

While shame begins to develop before we're cognizant, to become shame-based requires our intellectual cooperation. But God has given us a defense.

It is important to note that truth does not originate with the self. Self merely decides what it will accept as truth and then acts out of that belief. We always live life out of our core beliefs.

Self is like the goalkeeper of the heart. It makes judgments on all incoming information and decides which it will allow in and which it will deflect. The goal of this chapter is to discover the cause (the thought process) of shame so that we can be more skilled in our deflection of false information.

A Closer Look at the Problem

False shame reared its head at the very beginning of time. It was Satan's tactic in the first temptation. When we understand it there, we will understand it in every area of life. The story of God's provision of life for Adam and Eve is found in Genesis 2:8-9,15-17. The tree of life represented God Himself.

Adam was instructed to partake of this tree (thus feeding on the life of God), along with the other fruit-bearing trees in the garden, except one—

the tree of the knowledge of good and evil. This tree represented independence from God and the choice to live by one's own understanding. This was Satan's goal: If Adam and Eve chose it as their source of life, the world system would be established over which Satan, the god of this age, would rule (see 1 John 2:15-16; 5:19).

In Genesis 3:1-6, Satan tempted Eve to eat of the forbidden tree, and we see that he ensnared her with the power of false shame. He said, "If you eat of this tree, your eyes will be opened and you will be like God, knowing good and evil" (see verse 5).

Implication: To be fulfilled and successful in life, you need to be more than you are. Someone else (in this case, God) is higher and greater than you and this is not acceptable. You are deficient. The God who made you cannot be trusted to make you enough. The tree of life—God's life—is insufficient for the task. What you need is something from the world—the tree of the knowledge of good and evil—to make you enough. This is the shame message:

- You are not enough;
- God is not enough to make you enough;
- You need something from the world (something from your own understanding) to make you enough.

The first statement is true. But Satan loves to mix lies in with truth. In ourselves we are not enough. We are created to live dependent on God. The next two statements are pure lies.

Through the centuries Satan's message hasn't changed, and neither has his purpose. Satan's goal, then as now, is to erode our confidence in God so that consequently, we:

- reject ourselves as God made us;
- take matters into our own hands;
- begin to shape our lives according to our own wisdom.

When we shape our lives according to our wisdom, we begin to add things to ourselves that look good. To us, good is whatever furthers our cause.

There is another critical aspect of shame here. Satan snared Eve by comparing her to God. "If you eat, you will be like God" (see verse 5) implies that she is not like Him and she should be. When she accepts this deceptive logic, she is moved to compete with Him. Comparison is the high-octane fuel of shame.

Satan uses it because it always causes us to become self-focused. When we get our eyes on ourselves, we inevitably come up short.

Think about this shame message. Are there specific areas in your life where you feel that in order to meet the acceptable standard, you are not enough? What are these areas? Describe the standard you are trying so hard to meet.

_____
_____
_____
_____
_____

From where did you derive this standard (media, peers, parents)?

_____
_____
_____
_____
_____
_____

Ultimately, who is the source of the standard?

_____
_____
_____
_____
_____

How does it make you feel to realize that this standard is Satan's lie and is not what God intended at all?

_____
_____
_____
_____
_____
_____

A Closer Look at God's Truth

The cause of false shame is the lie of the shame message: "You are not enough. God is not enough to make you enough. You need something from the world, something from your own wisdom to make you enough." When we first hear this message, it is merely a temptation, not the result of sin we have committed. Note that false shame is the precursor to actual sin. As in Eve's case, it is Satan's attempt to move us out of God's provision for us.

Once we believe the lie, the temptation becomes sin in its most subtle form—the sin of unbelief. At this point, what we do to correct the perceived problem becomes overt sin and leads to legitimate shame. This will be discussed further in chapter 4.

What do 2 Corinthians 11:14 and Revelation 12:9 tell us that Satan does?

_____

_____

_____

_____

_____

Satan uses shame and guilt to accuse us. Shame locks us up inside ourselves and isolates us from others. Ultimately it is a prison of our own making, but we hold the key. Read Romans 12:2 and Proverbs 4:20-23. What do these verses tell us we have the power to do?

_____

_____

_____

_____

_____

What then should be our objective standard for truth?

_____

_____

_____

_____

_____

Read 2 Peter 1:3. How does this verse counter the shame message?

_____

_____

_____

_____

_____

_____

_____

A Closer Look at My Own Heart

When we believe the lie that we are not enough, that we should have something of goodness and excellence in ourselves, and that God has left something out of us that is essential to our wellbeing, we act on our own behalf. This is sin fulfilled—acted out—and ultimately leads to a legitimate sense of shame.

But for right now, we need to allow God to search our hearts.

Read Psalm 43:3 and Psalm 139:23. Ask God for discernment. What is true shame? What is false? Ask Him to show you the truth about Satan's lies, to give you the courage to see truth—God's truth—as He sees it.

_____

_____

_____

_____

_____

_____

_____

The *Amplified Bible*'s version of Psalm 25:2,4-5 can become your prayer.

O my God, I trust, lean on, rely on, and am confident in You. Let me not be put to shame or [my hope in You] be disappointed; let not my enemies triumph over me. Show me Your ways, O Lord; teach me Your paths. Guide me in Your truth and faithfulness and teach me, for You are the God of my salvation; for You [You only and altogether] do I wait [expectantly] all the day long.

Action Steps I Can Take Today

Write Psalm 25:2,4-5 on a card and put it in a place where you will see it often, such as the bathroom mirror, bedside table or over the kitchen sink. Meditate on it throughout the week. Share your verse with a friend. Ask him or her to pray with you as you begin to sort through Satan's lies. Take time to pray with one another.

PART TWO: COVERS FOR SHAME

Eve entered into the legitimate shame of sin when she believed Satan's lie that in order to be fulfilled and successful she needed to be more than she was. The God who made her could not be trusted to make her enough. She needed something from the world to make her complete; therefore, she acted on her own behalf.

Acting on our own behalf will take one of two forms: Either we will go into hiding in some form of withdrawal from life, or we will overtly cultivate qualities and accomplishments that we begin to trust as our entrance ticket into society—church included. The sin is not necessarily the activities themselves; some of them may be very good. The sin is trusting in them, whether good or evil, rather than God to make us acceptable to Him or to others.

Either of these forms of behavior is an attempt to protect our real selves from being exposed, rejected and ultimately abandoned. I call these behaviors "shame covers." We will next discuss what these covers are so that we can identify them in our own lives.

A Closer Look at the Problem

Following is a list of behaviors and activities that we often put on to cover our unacceptability—our nakedness. See if you can find any of the following in your closet:

WITHDRAWAL BEHAVIORS: HIDING THE DEFICIT
Avoiding social interaction. We often cover our unacceptability by avoiding social interaction, especially when it comes to sharing opinions and ideas. We're afraid others will think we're stupid. We decline opportunities to

serve on boards, committees and the like for which others think we're qualified. The give-and-take of thoughts and ideas threatens to expose too much of our inner selves to guarantee our safety.

Procrastination and indecisiveness. We're so afraid of doing it wrong or making wrong decisions that will expose our imperfection that we choose the safety of doing nothing until we have to do something.

Anesthetizing emotions. We anesthetize our emotions with addictive substances or behaviors such as alcohol, drugs, food, sex, shopping, TV and the like.

Self-occupied, overly self-relating and inward. This usually includes depression. We seem unable to get beyond our own self to care sincerely about others.

People-pleasing, nice all the time, few boundaries. We find that preventing conflict is more important, and safer, than honesty.

OVERT BEHAVIORS: MAKING UP (BUT STILL HIDING) THE DEFICIT

Increasingly social. We become active in multiple organizations, including church ministries, and may seek out leadership positions.

Investing much time and effort on outward appearance. Our value becomes in how we look to others.

Perfectionistic. This does not generally occur in every area, but just the ones in which we derive our identity (such as appearance, work, home or hobbies). We rationalize that if we can do a few things very well, maybe others won't notice how imperfect we really are.

Materialistic. What we have becomes what we are.

Humorous. We deflect anything or anyone who gets too close with a joke.

Overly involved. We become too involved in the lives of others or just plain busy all the time.

Intellectual. Our degrees begin to define who we are.

Extremely verbal. If we do all the talking, then we can control the conversation and ensure that it never gets too close to us.

Arrogant. We shame others and put them down in an attempt to convince them (and ourselves) that we are superior.

Controlling and rigid. This may include violent tendencies. We dominate our environment to ensure our own safety. Keeping others afraid makes confrontation and self-exposure less likely. Intermittent rage may be an effective weapon.

Rebellion. Refusing to meet the standard at school, work, home or in social situations is less painful than admitting we don't think we can meet it.

Religious, legalistic and judgmental. We exchange rules for personal relationship. What others do and what we do become more important than who we are.

Note that this list is far from complete. Can you think of other behaviors people engage in to cover themselves from perceived inadequacy? What are they?

_____

_____

_____

_____

_____

_____

_____

A Closer Look at God's Truth

Read Isaiah 30:1-3,5:

> Woe to the rebellious children, saith the LORD, that take counsel, but not of me; and that cover with a covering, but not of my spirit, that they may add sin to sin: That walk to go down into Egypt, and have not asked at my mouth; to strengthen themselves in the strength of Pharaoh, and to trust in the shadow of Egypt! Therefore shall the strength of Pharaoh be your shame, and the trust in the shadow of Egypt your confusion. They were all ashamed of a people that could not profit them, nor be an help nor profit, but a shame, and also a reproach (*KJV*).

What were the children of Israel refusing to do?

_____

_____

_____

_____

_____

_____

What were they doing instead?

_____

_____

_____

_____

_____

_____

What would be the end result?

_____

_____

_____

_____

_____

_____

In Scripture, Egypt is analogous to the world, and Pharaoh is analogous to Satan. Here we see the rebellious children going to the world for a covering rather than relying on God's Spirit. Isaiah says the result is that they "add sin to sin" (see Isaiah 30:1).

The first sin was not believing God would cover them. The second was going to the world to find their own covering. Consequently, instead of strength they found shame. Instead of protection they found confusion and reproach.

This is what happens when we reject God's provision for us. We go to the world to add what we think is missing. Even Christian activity becomes "of the world" when we trust in it as our means of acceptability. Anything apart from God Himself as our sufficiency is "of the world."

What we find out is that these things don't really cover us. Instead of resolving our shame they add to it. They are filthy rags and something inside of us knows it. Eventually we discover, just as Isaiah said we would, earlier in the same discourse: "[They will find that] the bed is too short for a man to stretch himself on and the covering too narrow for him to wrap himself in. [All their sources of confidence will fail them]" (Isaiah 28:20, AMP).

Think back to Adam and Eve in the garden. After they tried to do things their own way, they made for themselves their own covering. But it was not enough. Only clothing made as the result of a blood sacrifice could make them acceptable. Read Genesis 3:21. What did God do for Adam and Eve?

_____

_____

_____

_____

_____

_____

Read Revelation 1:5 and Isaiah 61:10. What has God done for you?

_____

_____

_____

_____

_____

_____

The deep pain of shame is the inner voice that says, *There is something wrong with you.* Righteousness is most simply defined as "made right." Read 2 Corinthians 5:18-21. How are we "made right"?

_____

_____

_____

_____

_____

Only the sacrifice of Christ on the cross for our sins is our covering and confidence before God and before others. What do the following verses tell you should be your confidence before people?

1 Corinthians 2:1-4

_____

_____

_____

_____

_____

Galatians 3:27

_____
_____
_____
_____
_____
_____

Galatians 6:14

_____
_____
_____
_____
_____
_____

A Closer Look at My Own Heart

Look back at the list of behaviors and activities that people "wear" to cover their own unacceptability (nakedness) in A Closer Look at the Problem (pages 36-38). Reread this list slowly and prayerfully. Did you find any coverings there that are part of your wardrobe?

In a short paragraph, describe the covering you wear most often.

_____
_____
_____
_____
_____
_____

Share an incident that shows you wearing it.

_____
_____
_____
_____
_____

Action Steps I Can Take Today

Making our own clothes erodes our strength because they keep wearing out. Styles—what's acceptable—keep changing as different environments require different coverings. We never feel as if we dress well enough for a new environment that requires another "style" of us. Read Isaiah 30:15. What does this verse tell you is the answer?

_____

_____

_____

_____

_____

_____

Write Isaiah 30:15 or another verse from this chapter that is meaningful to you on a card and post it alongside the verse from part one of this chapter. Meditate on your verses each day. Remember, the only way you can deflect Satan's lies is by using God's truth.

FOUR

$\mathscr{C}$ONTAGION OF SHAME (PART ONE)

Shame is contagious. People who live out of a shame base pass it on to others. It is, in fact, the pandemic disease of the world. It is the fuel that runs our economy. Having more, doing more, and being more are the life-blood of the advertising industry, and the propelling force behind many world powers. It isn't surprising that 1 John 5:19 tells us, "the whole world is under the control of the evil one" (*NIV*).

We can't do much about the whole world, but we *can* do something about ourselves. We can stop passing shame on to others.

This may be a difficult lesson to complete. People who grow up being shamed—that includes all of us to some degree—will shame others.

The goal of this chapter is to help us identify how we shame others. We'll also touch on the reasons why we shame others and examine the consequences of our behavior. We will look at the *why* of our conduct in greater detail in the next lesson.

A Closer Look at the Problem

Shame is the sense of feeling flawed, defective and unacceptable as a person. Therefore, this section could aptly be titled, "How We Contribute to Another's Sense of Feeling Flawed, Defective and Unacceptable as a Person."

The danger of reading a list like this is that it may cause us to feel more ashamed. This is not the purpose. Sometimes we don't recognize that we have shame until we see how we shame others. We have to know the uncomfortable truth about ourselves before we can be set free by the truth of God's Word.

We serve a redeeming, restoring God. With this in mind, take out a pen and your notebook. As you read, make a prayerful, private list of the shaming behaviors you identify with. Some of these are obviously shaming. Others are so subtle that all they take is a look, a movement or nothing at all. We'll consider both kinds.

OVERT SHAMING BEHAVIORS

Abuse. This could include physical, sexual, verbal or emotional abuse.

- *Physical abuse*: This is not limited to beatings but includes physical discipline applied in anger (such as spanking too hard, slapping the face, pulling hair or ears).

- *Sexual abuse*: This includes not only physical sexual violation but also inappropriate discussion, criticism or joking about another's private body parts. Includes telling sexual jokes, discussing details of one's own sexual behavior or acting in a sexually provocative manner in front of children or teenagers.

- *Verbal abuse*: This is not limited to name calling or swearing at someone but also includes labeling people instead of describing their actions—attacking the person instead of the problem. Continual criticism is also verbal abuse. It says, "There's only one right way—mine!"

- *Emotional Abuse:* Defined in all of the behaviors on this list.

Negating and shaming emotions and thoughts. This includes statements such as, "You shouldn't feel angry"; "Big girls/boys don't cry"; or "You shouldn't think like that." The message these statements portray is that feelings are weak and bad and that we are weak and bad for having them.

Spiritual browbeating. An example of this would be asking ourselves, *What would Jesus think about what we just did?* The message such statements send is that God only cares about what we *do* and that the real issues of our hearts are unimportant.

Disguising criticism or insults with humor. Statements such as "I was only joking!" puts all the blame for the humiliating or angry response on the other person.

Hammering away at topics long after the case has been made. The message this sends is, "You are an imbecile. You just don't get it!"

Comparing with others. This sends a message to others that they are not enough.

Shaming others with our own shame. Examples include over-disciplining children or overreacting in anger toward a spouse because his or her behavior embarrasses our already shame-based identity. We can't see our identity as separate from theirs.

Caretaking. This involves taking too much responsibility for others—doing things for them that they should be doing for themselves—which takes away their power and prevents maturity. This also includes keeping an account of another's spiritual growth (prayer life, Bible reading, and so forth).

Emotional neglect; not caring enough. Not taking time or giving enough attention to the people in our sphere of responsibility—such as children, spouse, parents. The message this sends is that they are not worthy of our attention; that there is something wrong with them.

Physical neglect. This includes financial irresponsibility, so that reasonable physical needs in the family are not being met. Also includes keeping a dirty, slovenly house, unkempt clothes and/or careless personal appearance. These types of behaviors send the message to our spouse and children that we don't care enough about them to provide them with a reasonable place to live.

Withholding affection. Includes not touching, or touching only when sex is on the agenda. This makes the other an object, not a person, and sends the message that his or her value is in what he or she can do for us.

SUBTLE SHAMING BEHAVIORS

Body language cues, such as rolling our eyes in disgust or shaking our head while others are speaking.

Interrupting others. This sends the message that our opinion is more important than the other person's.

Laughter or teasing. Laughing at serious remarks or smirking while another is talking.

Lack of eye contact. Not looking at others when they speak or appearing bored and uninterested. Some go so far as to turn up the volume on the TV so that they can hear it better when another is talking.

No response at all. No answer or acknowledgement that the other person has been heard.

CONSEQUENCES OF SHAMING

In light of the way shame has caused you to respond in your life, how do you think shaming others would cause them to respond?

_____

_____

_____

_____

_____

_____

_____

Has shame increased or decreased your ability to develop intimate relationships with others?

_____

_____

_____

_____

_____

_____

_____

Is this what you want to reproduce in the lives of the people you touch?

_____

_____

_____

_____

_____

_____

_____

What do you want in those relationships?

_____

_____

_____

_____

_____

_____

A Closer Look at God's Truth

Read Proverbs 12:4. This verse makes a powerful statement about a wife's relationship with her husband. "Bones" in Scripture are analogous to strength. Another word for rottenness is decay. What is this verse telling us?

_____

_____

_____

_____

_____

Read Genesis 2:23. This verse tells us that the woman is "bone of [her husband's] bone and flesh of [his] flesh." She is part of his own body. If a woman's behavior erodes and decays her husband's strength, what is she actually doing to herself?

_____

_____

_____

_____

_____

If a man's behavior shames his wife, what would be the effect on him?

_____

_____

_____

_____

_____

Shame weakens everybody—children, church family, community. Scripture tells us that believers are one Body. Ultimately, then, when we shame others, how does it affect us?

_____

_____

_____

_____

_____

Read 2 Samuel 6:20-23. What price did Michal pay for her contemptuous behavior toward David?

_____

_____

_____

_____

_____

_____

The term for having no children is "barren." Think about this word in a spiritual sense. What does it mean to you?

_____

_____

_____

_____

_____

_____

A Closer Look at My Own Heart

Take time to think about the implications of the list you made earlier (see pages 43-45). Perhaps there are other actions or behaviors you would like to add below.

_____

_____

_____

_____

_____

_____

_____

_____

When you are finished, lay your list alongside 1 John 1:6-10. Invite Jesus to guide you as you evaluate your list in the light of His Word.

Action Steps I Can Take Today

To walk in the light connotes transparency, honesty and truth. Write a transparent, honest and truthful prayer to the Lord concerning your list.

_____
_____
_____
_____
_____
_____
_____
_____

Read again what 1 John 1:7,9 tells us will be the result of this action. Take God at His word.

CONTAGION OF SHAME (PART TWO)

In the last chapter we learned that shame is contagious. We also learned some of the reasons why that is, and then evaluated our behavior in the light of God's Word. We can stop passing shame on! In this chapter we'll learn more about the *why* of our shaming behavior. The goal is to help us break the shame cycle of our lives.

A Closer Look at the Problem

The why of our behavior in this area is probably the same as it is in any other area. From our limited viewpoint, we think there is a payoff in it, some kind of benefit. Let's look at what some of our reasons might be and what we think we gain.

- *Ignorance*: For some people, the why is simply that they don't know they're doing it. Because of the subtlety of shame in our own lives, we have been unaware of its presence. Since it has seemed normal to talk to ourselves in shameful ways, we have been ignorant of the ways we communicate these same messages to others, especially those closest to us. If we don't know what shame is, we won't know we're passing it on. Regardless of our ignorance, however, it is still serving us in some way.

- *Frustration*: We see shame as a means to an end; it appears to be a way to affect change. Maybe, if we can make people—especially spouses and children—feel bad enough about themselves, they will do the good thing we're asking. Outwardly, they may comply; but inwardly, we'll drive them farther and farther away. Shaming another can seem good to us because what we want them to do is a good thing.

- *To gain power and control:* If we weaken others' self-confidence by a consistent barrage of shame messages, we automatically put ourselves on top.

- *Self-defense:* Shame seems like the logical response when we're shamed by someone else. It can also be used as a show of strength to keep others at a distance.

- *Habit:* We may know it's wrong but have never been confronted by someone who would no longer tolerate our bad behavior—so we keep doing it. We enjoy the sense of one-upmanship that it provides.

- *To shift attention from our own inadequacy:* If we can keep the focus on others' shortcomings, we don't have to face our own. Blame-shifting also comes in here: My shortcomings are their fault. If my husband/children/coworkers would do/look/feel better, then I would do/look/feel better. Or, if my husband would go to church, I could be a better Christian. If my children would mind me better, I wouldn't yell so much. If we could afford a nicer house, I would be a better housekeeper.

As we review the list of results we hoped to gain by shaming others, we can see how skewed and shortsighted our perspective has been. If the shame message in our own lives didn't produce healthy, whole people, it is obvious that inflicting it on others won't either. The reality is that no one is helped.

But that's not all the bad news. There is also great loss to us. As we learned in chapter 4, the payback far outweighs the payoff.

A Closer Look at God's Truth

Shame is perpetuated in a cyclical fashion. We are shamed, we shame others, they shame us, ad infinitum. The result of shame, whether we are the victim or the perpetrator, is distance and hiding from relationships. Shame robs us of our ability to be intimate with others.

One person can break the shame cycle in his or her own environment by committing to, and setting up, an "intimacy cycle." This simply means that we can determine to become real and respectful in the presence of others, even when they are not. We can begin to become a place of safety so that—in time—they, too, might dare to become real with us and others. (To help you further understand these cycles, there is an illustration of the intimacy/shame cycles on page 95 of the leader's guide.)

This commitment takes great courage. It requires the willingness to become naked in the face of danger, and open to possible betrayal and rejection. It can be done only when we find a personal security and safety so powerful that we no longer need to provide it for ourselves.[1]

Read John 13:1-5. Jesus is washing the disciples' feet the night before His betrayal and crucifixion. What did Jesus know that enabled Him to humbly serve His disciples in this intimate way? Write down four things you discover from verse 3 that Jesus knew about Himself.

_____

_____

_____

_____

_____

Because Jesus knew these things, He had nothing left to prove. Knowing who His Father was, where He had come from, where He was going, and that the Father had given all things into His hands, He did not need to depend upon His own covering for significance. His identity was in His relationship to—and with—the Father. Jesus' work, carrying out the Father's business, was simply an outflow of His intimate knowledge of the Father's heart. As a mature son, He had a sense of ownership of the Father's purposes. Secure in who He was, He removed His garments, put on a servant's towel and washed the dirt of the world from the disciples' feet, a humble but intimate act (see verses 4-5).

Now read John 13:14-17. What do these verses tell us we are to do?

_____

_____

_____

_____

_____

If we are to do what He did, then we have to know what He knew. Can what was said about Him be said of us? Why or why not?

_____

_____

_____

_____

_____

_____

Read the following verses that refer to us and correlate them with what you have learned about Jesus in John 13:

John 14:2-3

_____

_____

_____

_____

_____

_____

_____

John 20:17

_____

_____

_____

_____

_____

_____

Galatians 4:4-7

_____

_____

_____

_____

_____

_____

1 John 4:4,6

_____
_____
_____
_____
_____
_____
_____

A Closer Look at My Own Heart

Will the truth that was enough for Jesus be enough for you? Why or why not?

_____
_____
_____
_____
_____
_____
_____
_____

Action Steps I Can Take Today

Read Ephesians 1:15-23. Although Paul prayed these verses for others, they are God's will for every believer. Paraphrase them into a prayer for your own needs. For example, "Glorious Father, I ask You to give me the Spirit of wisdom and revelation that I might know you better. Open the eyes of my heart that I might . . ."

_____
_____
_____
_____
_____
_____

Make a commitment to call a friend—someone in your group or a friend who prays for and with you. Pray Paul's prayer for each other over the phone.

Note

1. If you are in a relationship with a history of physical violence, even respectful, honest communication can trigger an attack. It would be best to do your serious talking in the presence of a third party, i.e., pastor or counselor.

Cure for Shame (Part One)

We are designed for intimacy; to know and be known by God and others is meant to be the core of our existence. It is out of such intimate knowledge that true love is born. True love brings an authentic, transparent self to others, but shame robs us of that ability.

- Shame drives us into hiding so that we can neither be known nor truly loved.
- Shame prevents us from knowing and loving others.
- Shame is the thief that steals intimacy.

Shame is lived out in darkness. Its cave is the secret, barricaded and sealed recesses of our heart and mind. Its food is the lies and half-truths of the accuser himself—the one whose total reason for existence is to destroy or, at the very least, incapacitate God's dearest creation (see John 10:10). The boulder rolled in front of the door is the BIG lie: "You can't trust God."

The goal of this chapter is to confront some of the lesser, but still immobilizing, lies that Satan tells us. In chapter 7 we'll dynamite the big stone, the one that paralyzes us and makes the other lies seem logical.

A Closer Look at the Problem

What we're calling lesser lies all have their root in the same soil: comparison and the resulting competition. Comparison says:

- *Difference is bad.* The only interpretation for difference is good or bad, better or worse, right or wrong. It's risky being different. You might come up short in someone's eyes—most painfully, your own. If you can't be better, at least be the same.

- *Limited is defective.* Everyone should have it all and be all. You must not fall short in anything. Creating a life of independence from others is the key to happiness and safer than the risk of being disappointed by them.

- *Perfect is the only acceptable standard.* Anything less than perfection disqualifies you as an acceptable human being.

- *Your value is assessed by the world's standard.* How well you measure up to, or better yet, exceed others in possessions, looks, position or intelligence determines your worth.

A Closer Look at God's Truth

Comparison and competition strike at the very heart of God's design for His Church. (Surprise! Surprise!) They are actually Satan's twisted version of God's pattern—contrast and completion. Let's restate these four lies in their truthful form. For each statement, there are questions, commentary, and/or Scripture for you to discuss.

TRUTH: DIFFERENCE IS GOOD!

God is a God of difference. He has created a world of differences: colors, snowflakes, fingerprints, races, gender. It is the contrast of differences that completes the whole. The differences between male and female complete one flesh. The differences in the Body of Christ make up the full expression of His nature.

Rather than seeing yourself through the eyes of comparison and competition, look at yourself instead through the eyes of *contrast* and *completion*. Do you see spiritual truths more in picture form, as in stories from nature, rather than a scholarly approach? Is it possible that there are whole groups of people whose ability to grasp truth is more geared to your approach than the other?

Do you wish you were more social, charismatic and outgoing? Could it be that God's gifting in your life depends on your ability to be quiet and spend large quantities of time alone?

Can you think of an area in your life that, while it may have a different expression than those areas of the people around you, may be a part of the whole? Briefly describe that area.

_____
_____
_____
_____
_____
_____

If you are married, spend some time making a list of the differences between you and your spouse. What dissimilarities do you observe that contrast your personalities and thus complete the whole?

_____
_____
_____
_____
_____
_____

TRUTH: LIMITED IS GOD'S DESIGN
Read 1 Corinthians 10:16-17. The communion of fellowship in the body and blood of Christ is a shared one—each person partakes from one loaf. How is the loaf made whole again?

_____
_____
_____
_____
_____

How does this truth apply to you?

_____
_____
_____
_____
_____

God declares that the Church corporately is the fullness of God (see Ephesians 4:13). That means that none of us has it all and that's the way it's meant to be. We each bring different gifts and talents that together express His character. God designed the Church to function in such a manner that each of us is a part of the whole. Interdependence is God's plan.

Although all believers are given a measure of faith, none of us has all the gifts. One woman berates herself because she finds it difficult to organize a simple buffet without a lot of stress. On the other hand she can sit for hours at the bedside of a sick friend.

Read Romans 12:3-8. What gift do you think this woman might have?

_____

_____

_____

_____

_____

_____

What gift doesn't she have?

_____

_____

_____

_____

_____

_____

How does she illustrate the truth that what we sometimes interpret as unacceptable about ourselves is merely valid evidence of our limitation and is part of God's plan?

_____

_____

_____

_____

_____

_____

Reread verse 3. What word do you think of that encapsulates the meaning of "Thinking more highly of ourselves than we ought"?

_____

_____

_____

_____

_____

_____

It is only when we believe we should be more than God has made us that we become ashamed of our limitations. Shame is actually the flipside of pride.

Respond to this verse: "When pride comes, then comes shame; but with the humble is wisdom" (Proverbs 11:2).

_____

_____

_____

_____

_____

_____

_____

TRUTH: PERFECTION IS A CONDITION WE'RE MOVING TOWARD THROUGH THE GRACE OF GOD

For now, perfection is limited to God and eternity. While we are told in Matthew 5:48 that we are to be perfect, this verse must be placed in the context of the whole of Scripture.

Read the following verses and write down what you conclude about your present condition here on earth:

Luke 8:15

_____

_____

_____

_____

_____

_____

Philippians 1:6

_____

_____

_____

_____

_____

_____

_____

Philippians 3:12-14

_____

_____

_____

_____

_____

_____

_____

Hebrews 13:20-21

_____

_____

_____

_____

_____

_____

_____

James 1:2-4

_____

_____

_____

_____

_____

_____

_____

Read Romans 15:4-7. How should knowing that we are a people in process, that we are not yet perfect and will not be in this lifetime, affect our attitude toward ourselves and others?

_____

_____

_____

_____

_____

_____

TRUTH: YOUR VALUE AND SIGNIFICANCE ARE IN YOUR IDENTITY
Only the God who created us can tell us who we are. Read the following Scriptures and write down what you discover about your own identity. According to these verses, who does God say you are?

Ephesians 2:10

_____

_____

_____

_____

_____

_____

1 Peter 2:5-9

_____

_____

_____

_____

_____

_____

1 John 3:1-2

_____

_____

_____

_____

_____

_____

Revelation 1:6

_____

_____

_____

_____

A Closer Look at My Own Heart

God has blended your personality with your individual strengths and weaknesses, your talents, spiritual gifts and interests, even your environment and heritage, into a person that is uniquely you. Prayerfully ask yourself, "What is there about me that makes me unique?" You may wish to use your notebook or journal for your responses.

What is my personality?

_____

_____

_____

_____

_____

What are my talents?

_____

_____

_____

_____

_____

My interests?

_____

_____

_____

_____

_____

What do I think might be my spiritual gift(s)?

_____

_____

_____

_____

_____

_____

What is my greatest strength?

_____

_____

_____

_____

_____

_____

My greatest weakness?

_____

_____

_____

_____

_____

_____

How has God used me to minister to someone this week?

_____

_____

_____

_____

_____

_____

Action Steps I Can Take Today

Ponder this truth: Just as my fingerprints are unique to me, so I am unique in the Body of Christ. Because God has created and gifted me to function in a place prepared especially for me, I don't have to wait to become something more in order to minister to somebody. I can start today. Ask God to bring into your mind something you can do for somebody else. Then do it!

SEVEN

CURE FOR SHAME (PART TWO)

In chapter 6 we explored the four little lies Satan uses to disable us and keep us from experiencing intimacy with God and others. These lies are:

1. Difference is bad.
2. Limited is defective.
3. Perfect is the only acceptable standard.
4. Our value is assessed by how well we measure up to the world's standard.

In this chapter, we'll look at what gives credence to these little lies. It is the *big lie* sitting at the front door of our hearts. On it is written, "You can't trust God."

A Closer Look at the Problem

Satan's lie, that God can't be trusted, gives birth to the root of all sin: unbelief in God. The Israelites couldn't enter the Promised Land, the fullness of God's provision for them, because of unbelief (see Hebrews 3:12-19). In fact, these verses say we have wicked hearts of unbelief (see verse 12). If we don't believe that God is enough for our existence in this world, that His life is all we need to be acceptable to Him and others, then we are robbed of the very source of our life. There is no other life (see Deuteronomy 30:19-20).

Hebrews 3:10 gives the reason for the Israelites' distrust in God. It says they didn't know His ways—in reality, they didn't know Him. This is the cause of distrust in all of us. We can neither trust nor love someone we don't know. Nor can we believe he loves us.

We can say we love God and yet not really know Him. The Israelites followed God in the desert for 40 years, yet Psalm 103:7 tells us they only knew His *acts*. But Moses knew His *ways*. He knew God's heart. This is what we need to know if we are going to trust Him enough to let go of our own strategies of self-protection.

To know God's heart is to know what He is doing, what He has been working toward from the beginning. To discover this, we'll divide our search into three sections: First, "Who Is God? What Is He Like?" Second, "What Was His Plan from the Beginning?" Third, "What Drove Him to Such Lengths to Fulfill His Plan?"

A Closer Look at God's Truth

The deception of shame is that God is an angry God, a hard taskmaster who has no patience with imperfection. This is how the Israelites saw God. Not so Moses.

Who Is God? What Is He Like?

Read Exodus 33:12-13,18-23. When Moses became aware that God knew him by name, what request did he make of God (verses 13,18)?

_____

_____

_____

_____

_____

_____

What was God's response?

_____

_____

_____

_____

_____

Read Exodus 34:5-7. God Himself told Moses what He is really like. Correlate verse 7 with Exodus 20:5-6, which says God shows mercy to those who love Him and visits iniquity on those who hate Him. What do these verses tell us is the nature of God?

_____
_____
_____
_____
_____
_____

From these verses we see that God is love and what the nature of His love is. We also see that He is a relational God who wants to be known. He was pleased with Moses' request to know Him and responded by revealing to him His own personal name, Jehovah, or *Yahweh* in Hebrew.

"Name" denotes honor, authority, character.[1] In Exodus 6:2-3, God told Moses that his forefathers had known Him as God Almighty; but by His name, LORD (Jehovah), He did not make Himself known to them.

Now God makes His name (His nature, who He really is) known to someone for the first time. The qualities that follow His name are God's description of His own character.

Moses' request to know God as intimately as he was known by God was the response of a maturing son. If God was pleased to respond to Moses' request to know Him, how do you think He would respond to yours?

_____
_____
_____
_____
_____
_____

Read 1 John 4:8,16. Who do these verses tell you God is?

_____
_____
_____
_____
_____
_____

Who is the object of His love?

_____

_____

_____

_____

_____

Respond to this statement: "True love reveals itself."

_____

_____

_____

_____

_____

WHAT WAS GOD'S PLAN FROM THE BEGINNING?

From the beginning, God intended to have a people for His own possession. As a Father whose nature is love, He wanted "sons"—male and female—who would be the objects of that love. When God refers to "sons" in the Old and New Testaments in reference to His people, the term not only incorporates male and female but also denotes the quality of one growing toward maturity (see Galatians 3:26–4:7 in the *NKJV, NIV, NASB* or *AMP* versions).

God planned that these offspring would have the capacity to know Him, understand His heart, fellowship with Him, and because of that relationship, represent Him to a watching universe (see Ephesians 3:10). This is what He was saying when He declared, "Let us make man in our image, in our likeness, and let them rule" (Genesis 1:26, *NIV*).

Image means "representative figure."[2] Therefore, we were created to represent Him in His likeness. To be like Him, we would have to know Him.

To have a people who would know His heart—that He is an omnipotent God moved by a fierce, unswerving, unfailing love toward those He has made for Himself—has always been the center of God's plan. This is the goal of everything He does.

Read 2 Peter 1:2-3 (*AMP*):

> May grace (God's favor) and peace (which is perfect well-being, all
> necessary good, all spiritual prosperity, and freedom from fears

and agitating passions and moral conflicts) be multiplied to you in [the full, personal, precise, and correct] knowledge of God and of Jesus our Lord. For His divine power has bestowed upon us all things that [are requisite and suited] to life and godliness, through the [full, personal] knowledge of Him Who called us by and to His own glory and excellence (virtue).

God has promised us peace and rest in this life. From what do these verses tell us our peace will be derived?

_____
_____
_____
_____
_____
_____
_____

How has God provided for our life of godliness (God-likeness)? Also see 2 Corinthians 3:18.

_____
_____
_____
_____
_____
_____

What "things" does 2 Peter 1:3 tell us God has provided for our life and godliness?

_____
_____
_____
_____
_____
_____
_____
_____

What things do we need to add to ourselves?

_____

_____

_____

_____

_____

_____

What we are to do (love God and others) should be an automatic outflow of
who we are—"sons" who know their Father. The deception of shame is that
it causes us to focus on ourselves. God's provision is that we focus on Him.
Read Ephesians 1:3-6. According to these verses, when were we chosen?

_____

_____

_____

_____

_____

_____

Why were we chosen? Give at least three reasons.

_____

_____

_____

_____

_____

_____

Through whom does God achieve His purpose?

_____

_____

_____

_____

_____

_____

WHAT DROVE GOD TO SUCH LENGTHS TO FULFILL HIS PLAN?
It is important to note that God didn't create us because of what we would
do for Him, what we would be in ourselves, or even fundamentally because

we would love Him. First John 4:10 says, "In this is love, not that we loved God, but that He loved us."

God created us out of His love, for His own glory and to satisfy the longing of His own heart for children who could share in His life.

We know that God's plan to have a people for Himself came under immediate attack. A great catastrophe happened—mankind fell. But God has never been diverted from His determinate course.

The remedy for the Fall was in place before the first star was hung in the sky. The essence of the book of Hebrews is that we can rest in assurance that all God has planned will come to pass because the works were finished since the foundation—the very thought or conception—of the world. In God's economy, the plan was fulfilled before it started. Now He simply asks us to believe Him for it (see Hebrews 4:3).

Read John 1:29 and Revelation 13:8b. Describe God's remedy for the Fall in your own words.

_____

_____

_____

_____

_____

_____

A Closer Look at My Own Heart

Jesus is the Lamb of God, slain from the foundation of the world. Read Matthew 18:11-14 and ponder this thought: *If I had been the only person in the world who needed a redeemer, Jesus would have died for me.*

What was it that moved Him to do this for you?

_____

_____

_____

_____

_____

_____

How would you like this truth to transform your life?

_____

_____

_____

_____

_____

_____

Action Steps I Can Take Today

How has this lesson made a difference in the way you view yourself?

_____

_____

_____

_____

_____

_____

How has it made a difference in the way you view God?

_____

_____

_____

_____

_____

_____

Tell someone about it.

Notes

1. James Strong, *Strong's Exhaustive Concordance of the Bible* (Nashville, TN: Thomas Nelson Publishers, 1990), #8034, p. 731.
2. Ibid., #6754, p. 528.

CURE FOR SHAME (PART THREE)

The heart of the message of this study on shame could be summarized in this way: The cure for false shame (that deep, nagging sense of inadequacy communicated through the shame message) and its successor, legitimate shame (resulting from the sin of believing the lie and acting on our own behalf to make up the deficit), is *knowing the love of the Father*!

The first lesson on the cure for shame in chapter 6 helped us see how Satan's little lies barricade our hearts against the love of God and others. The second lesson in chapter 7 dynamited the *big lie* that gave birth to all the little lies. We can trust God!

Why? Because He loved us so much that He put His plan for our redemption and restoration into action even before the creation of the world. The goal of this, our final chapter, is to more fully experience that love.

A Closer Look at the Problem

God sent Jesus to die for us "in order to satisfy the great and wonderful and intense love with which He loved us" (Ephesians 2:4, *AMP*). As a faithful creator, the love that created us would not rest until the way back to Himself was fully open.

Jesus' death for us was the ultimate demonstration of God's unswerving commitment to the children He had made for Himself. It was the only way He could get His family back. It was the supreme expression of the depth of His love. There is no greater love than this (see John 15:13).

But there was more—the seal of His love, His crowning provision, the intended culmination of all He had done—He "sent forth the Spirit of His Son into your hearts, crying out, 'Abba, Father!' " (Galatians 4:6). The Father's plan had been realized—God's Spirit in the heart of man so He can

be known. "This is [My] covenant . . . all shall know Me, from the least . . .
to the greatest" (Hebrews 8:10-12).

A Closer Look at God's Truth

Read Deuteronomy 7:6-8; Isaiah 63:7-9; John 3:16; 15:13; Romans 5:8;
Ephesians 2:4-7; Titus 3:4-5 and 1 John 3:16; 4:9.What do we find declared
over and over as God's reason for redeeming us?

_____

_____

_____

_____

_____

What point is God making by giving us so many statements concerning
His great love?

_____

_____

_____

_____

_____

_____

Read Ephesians 2:18. What does this verse say about us?

_____

_____

_____

_____

_____

Through whom do we have access?

_____

_____

_____

_____

_____

Christ is our covering—in Him we are enough. In Him we've already become what we need to be: "the righteousness of God in Him [Christ]" (2 Corinthians 5:21). Daily life is simply the process God uses to work out in our experience what He has already done. Read Genesis 1:26-27 and Romans 8:28-29. What do these verses tell us God is doing in us?

_____

_____

_____

_____

_____

_____

_____

In this study we have stated that the shame message, once believed, drives us to the world to find our own covering. This is a way of saying that we love the world, that we choose the things that are pleasant to the eyes, are good for food and enhance our pride of life, over the Father (see Genesis 3:6; 1 John 2:16). Read 1 John 2:15-16. Notice that verse 15 doesn't say, "If anyone loves the world, he doesn't have love for the Father." What does it really say?

_____

_____

_____

_____

_____

_____

_____

The only reason people go to the world for their comfort and significance is because they don't yet know the love of the Father or the sure hope of His calling. They don't know His powerful, unfailing love for them or that He has already accomplished all they need for life and godliness. He has left nothing out.

Read Ephesians 3:14-21 several times. This passage describes the Father's love as revealed in Jesus in one of the most beautiful and unforgettable prayers in the Bible. It is a prayer Paul prayed for the Ephesians. From whom does the whole family in heaven and earth derive its name (nature, character)?

_____

_____

_____

_____

_____

Even though families often fall short of God's intention, God has placed within each of us something that instinctively knows what families should be. The nature of the family—the protection, provision and nurturing jointly ministered through mothers and fathers; the sense of belonging, of intimately knowing and being known; the trustful dependence of the children—all issue forth from the fatherhood of God.

Reread verses 17-19. What is to be the very soil of a Christian's existence?

_____

_____

_____

_____

_____

What do the terms "rooted" and "grounded" mean to you?

_____

_____

_____

_____

_____

What is the result of being rooted and grounded in Christ's love?

_____

_____

_____

_____

_____

Who gets the glory?

_____

_____

_____

_____

_____

_____

CHALLENGE ACTIVITY

Read the first three chapters of Ephesians in one sitting. Note that the practical instructions that follow in chapters 4–6 flow out of the revelation of God the Father's accomplished plan to have sons for Himself as described in chapters 1–3. Our ability to love one another and walk in relationships springs out of the knowledge of our Father's love for us.

A Closer Look at My Own Heart

The cure for false shame (the deep, nagging sense of inadequacy communicated through the shame message) and its successor, legitimate shame (the result of sin), is knowing the love of the Father. In His love He has provided everything we need for life and godliness: acceptance, redemption, security, identity, purpose and worth. In addition, He has given us His own Holy Spirit that we may know Him and have power for living.

Here is a prayer to pray from your heart to the heart of your Father:

Father in heaven, we pray like Paul and Moses:
Father of glory, give me the spirit of wisdom and revelation in the deep and intimate knowledge of You. Open the eyes of my understanding so that I can know the hope to which I have been called and how rich Your glorious inheritance is in me so that I will no longer look to the weak and beggarly things of this world. Cause me to know how great and immeasurable and unlimited Your power is in me who believes. Show me Your glory, Lord, so that I will know You and thus become more and more like You. Lord, I accept Your grace that provides for the fact that I am a person in process. Help me give this same grace to others. In Jesus' name I pray. Amen.

Action Steps I Can Take Today

As you complete this Bible study, remember this: Your Father loves you. Everything from creation, to redemption, to restoring you to sonship has been done through Jesus Christ, to bring you to Himself that you may know Him. In His love and grace, "He has made us accepted in the beloved" (Ephesians 1:6, *KJV*). Post this simple but profound verse where you can see it every day. Through Christ, you are acceptable! As you journey through each day, let God's truth be your final arbiter.

And we know that the Son of God has come and has given us an understanding, that we may know Him who is true; and we are in Him who is true, in His Son Jesus Christ. This is the true God and eternal life.

1 JOHN 5:20

FROM SHAME TO BEAUTY LEADER'S GUIDE

The purpose of this leader's guide is to provide those willing to lead a group Bible study with additional material to make the study more effective. Each lesson has one or two exercises designed to increase participation and lead the group members into closer relationship with their heavenly Father.

Each of the exercises are designed to introduce the study and emphasize the theme of the chapter. When two exercises are suggested, it is up to your discretion whether to use them both. Time will probably be the deciding factor.

If the group is larger than six members, you may want to break into smaller groups for the discussion time so that all will have an adequate opportunity to share. As the lessons proceed, the exercises will invite more personal sharing. Keep these two important points in mind:

1. Involve each member of the group in the discussion when at all possible. Some may be too shy or new to the Bible study experience. Be sensitive to their needs and encourage them to answer simple questions that do not require personal information or biblical knowledge. As they get more comfortable in the group, they will probably share more often.

2. Make a commitment with the group members that what is shared in the discussion times and prayer requests must be kept in strictest confidence.

After each lesson, be prepared to pray with those who have special needs or concerns. Emphasize the truth of God's Word as you minister to the group members, which will lead them to a closer relationship with their Lord and Savior.

ONE

CONTRIBUTORS TO SHAME

Objective

To help group members personally identify contributing factors to the power of shame in their own lives.

Preparation

EXERCISE

Look through magazines and cut out ads that imply personal defectiveness will be resolved by the product being offered. Include some that are directed specifically toward women and some specifically toward men. If you wish, you might also write out some TV ads using this theme.

Some ads will be obvious (for instance, a dandruff shampoo ad that implies that having flakes on your shoulder will make you disgusting, but if you use their product you will be acceptable again), while others will be less obvious (for instance, an ad with a girl on the back of the motorcycle, implying that if the user buys this motorcycle he will automatically be attractive to beautiful women). Collect both kinds.

Also look for ads that imply normal is unacceptable (such as anti-aging cream ads) or that perfection is the normal standard (such as the ads featuring a perfectly proportioned woman clad in underwear that promises to correct figure flaws).

DISCUSSION

Familiarize yourself with the discussion questions included in the following "Group Participation" section. Note that there might not be time to discuss every question, so modify or adapt this discussion guide as it fits the needs of your group. Additional discussion/action steps are also provided for some chapters to help stimulate further discussion if you have the time.

Group Participation

EXERCISE

Give each group member one or more of the ads. Ask each to identify the shame message and share it with the others. You may want to read the TV advertising slogans you wrote down yourself.

DISCUSSION

1. Discuss the following questions from the "A Closer Look at God's Truth" section:

   • Romans 10:9-11 and Revelation 3:17-18 apply to legitimate shame that is the result of sin. What are we told is the answer to this awful dilemma?

   • Earlier we talked about false shame and how God never intended for His children to feel vulnerable, unclothed and fearful of rejection. Read Psalm 139:1-18. What do you discover about yourself before you were even born?

   • What are some of the truths that counter the lies you have been fed in Romans 8:28-29, Philippians 1:6 and Hebrews 13:20-21?

   • Make a thoughtful list of personal characteristics or events in your life, beginning with your childhood, that you believe contributed to negative self-judgments.

ADDITIONAL DISCUSSION/ACTION STEPS

Read the woman's story and Gary's story on pages 15-16 aloud to the group. Ask group members to follow along in their own books. Then discuss the following questions.

1. What truth about shame are these two people hearing? (*Shame is a bottomless pit. As soon as one imperfection is fixed, we discover another. We can never do enough to make ourselves perfect.*)

2. Do you have a personal experience similar to these individuals' stories that you would like to share with the group?

3. What are some examples of this phenomenon being lived out in some segments of our society? (*Continual plastic surgeries, breast implants, liposuction, and so forth.*)

TWO

CHARACTERISTICS OF SHAME

Objective

To help group members identify specific characteristics that have developed in response to the emotion of shame. We want to lead them into a more personal understanding of the lifelong effect shaming experiences can have.

Preparation

EXERCISE

Choose the most vivid memory of being shamed you can recall that you are willing to share. (It's all right if it is one you shared last week—we want to look more closely at it this time.) You may also want to refer to the woman's story from chapter 1 to illustrate the point of the exercise.

Group members may not be able to articulate their answers clearly at this point in the study. That's all right—our purpose, while using only one example, is to help them begin unraveling the connection between life experiences and their present feelings about themselves. While Satan is the author of false shame, he uses people and circumstances to perpetuate his lies.

We will add to this exercise in the next chapter, so read ahead in this guide to the exercise in chapter 3 so that you will understand how the two work together.

DISCUSSION

Familiarize yourself with the discussion questions included in the following "Group Participation" section.

Group Participation

EXERCISE

Share your memory of shame briefly with the group and include the following information:

- What this experience did inside of me

- What message it gave me about myself (what became truth to me about myself from that point on)

- How I feel when that part of me is exposed or threatened with exposure

Save this information for reference until chapter 3, at which time group members will be adding to these questions.

DISCUSSION

Discuss the following questions from the "A Closer Look at God's Truth" section:

- Paul declares in 1 Corinthians 6:20 and again in 7:23 that you were bought with a price. With these comments in mind, who must the merchant in the parable of Matthew 13:45-46 represent?

- Who are the pearls of great value?

- What is Jesus saying about us?

- Read John 3:16. How does it make you feel to realize that you are so valuable that the very God of the universe gave the life of His most valued possession (His Son, Jesus) to redeem you and buy you back for Himself?

- How did Ephesians 1:4-6, Ephesians 2:4-10 and 1 John 3:1 help you reassess who you are?

*C*AUSE AND COVERS FOR SHAME

Objective

To help group members become more skilled at identifying the messages of shame and to help them identify specific behaviors they thought were innate to their personality but, in reality, may be responses to feelings of shame.

Preparation

EXERCISE 1

Make a list of specific qualities or standards that society sets up to determine our acceptability (size 6 figure, no "lumps," beautiful hair, college graduate, home owner, married, and so forth). Include the standards the Church also communicates to us that, in reality, have nothing to do with our relationship with Christ (articulate speaker, financially comfortable, stay-at-home mom, and the like). The purpose of this exercise is to make group members more aware of (1) the constant barrage of messages that snare us into comparing ourselves with others, and (2) how very narrow and limited the sphere of acceptability is, or in other words, how little room there is for differences among individuals.

EXERCISE 2

Write the names of the following "masks" on a whiteboard, chalkboard or flipchart:

- Monster
- Witch
- John Wayne
- Lone Ranger/Zorro

- Fairy Godmother
- Princess
- Clown
- Genie
- Marilyn Monroe
- Sasquatch/Big Foot

DISCUSSION

Familiarize yourself with the discussion questions included in the following "Group Participation" section, or choose which questions in the study you would like to discuss with the group.

Group Participation

EXERCISE 1

Have the group make a list according to the above directions, saving your own contributions until the end. Add any from your collection that were missing from the group's suggestions. Ask the following questions:

- How do these standards affect the way you feel about yourself?
- How have they affected your willingness to participate with others?

EXERCISE 2

Show the group the list of masks—good, evil and in between—that you wrote on the whiteboard, chalkboard or flipchart. These are masks that some of the group members might have worn as children on Halloween, and each has a connotation applicable to this lesson. The goal of this exercise is to bring awareness to the fact that while there are good masks (behaviors) and bad masks, they are all still masks that we use to hide from others.

Name the masks individually and ask the group to describe the persona suggested by the mask. Use the descriptions given below if they are missed, and feel free to add your own thoughts as well.

- Monster: scary, intimidating, aggressive, threatening
- Witch: critical, sharp-tongued
- John Wayne: strong, but relationally independent
- Lone Ranger/Zorro: rescuer, always helping others but never allowing himself to be known (Who was that masked man?)

- Fairy Godmother: all-powerful, seems to know what is good for everyone else, always meeting the needs of others but has no needs of her own
- Princess: lacks nothing, best of everything, perfectionist who seeks preeminence; she would rather be admired than known (which is true of many of these masks)
- Clown: always joking; uses humor to keep people from getting too close
- Genie: the people-pleasing mask; exists to serve others (Your wish is my command.)
- Marilyn Monroe: dependent on appearance (How I look is my ticket of admittance into society.)
- Sasquatch/Big Foot: shy, hidden, afraid of others; may appear humble as a mask for fear

Ask the group if any of the masks—whether good, evil, or somewhere in between—are more or less deceptive than the others. What is the true purpose of the masks? (*To hide our true identity*.)

DISCUSSION

1. As time allows, discuss the following questions (or the ones you chose) from Part One of the study:

   - What do 2 Corinthians 11:14 and Revelation 12:9 tell us that Satan does?

   - Read Romans 12:2 and Proverbs 4:20-23. What do these verses tell us we have the power to do?

   - What then should be our objective standard for truth?

   - Read 2 Peter 1:3. How does this verse counter the shame message?

   - Read Psalm 43:3 and Psalm 139:23. Ask God for discernment. What is true shame? What is false? Ask Him to show you the truth about Satan's lies, to give you the courage to see truth—God's truth—as He sees it.

2. As time allows, discuss the following questions (or the ones you chose) from Part Two of the study:

- Read Isaiah 30:1-3,5. What were the children of Israel refusing to do?

- What were they doing instead?

- What would be the end result?

- Read Genesis 3:21. What did God do for Adam and Eve?

- Read 2 Corinthians 5:18-21. How are we "made right"?

- Describe the covering you wear most often.

- Share an incident that shows you wearing it.

ADDITIONAL DISCUSSION/ACTION STEPS

1. Ask the group what things or qualities they admired in others while growing up that they thought made these individuals more acceptable than them. This could include a wide range of things. For example, if a person's family didn't have much money for extras, it could be something like having Christmas lights on their house, having two bathrooms, having a ring with a real jewel in it, having certain kinds of clothes (or lots of clothes) or having a particular kind of pet (a poodle or a boxer instead of a mutt). If a person's family was financially comfortable, it could be another person's perceived quality of his or her family life.

2. Ask the members how this has influenced the choices they've made in their adult lives. That is, are they aware of adding things to their lives—perhaps even unconsciously—that were a direct result of believing those things would make them as acceptable as the people whom they admired?

FOUR

CONTAGION OF SHAME
(PART ONE)

Objective

To help group members personally identify shaming behaviors and how they pass them on to others.

Preparation

EXERCISE 1

Shaming behavior is learned. It is also a truism that "hurt people hurt people." Think about and prepare a short presentation describing your own childhood and shaming behaviors that were acted out toward you. If you can, identify and share with the group what it was in the life experience of these people who displayed these shaming behaviors that caused them to become shame "carriers" (someone who passes a disease along to others).

EXERCISE 2

On a whiteboard, chalkboard or flipchart, make a list of the many TV sitcoms and children's programs that use shame as the main fuel for getting laughs.

DISCUSSION

Familiarize yourself with the discussion questions included in the following "Group Participation" section.

Group Participation

EXERCISE 1

Ask others to share briefly some experiences where they were shamed and, if they are able, what they think contributed to their perpetrator's behavior. Set a time limit for this exercise.

EXERCISE 2

Show the group the list of TV shows you created (ask for other contributions) to discuss the type of behavior that is being held up as acceptable, even desirable, in our society today. Ask, "What is it about this behavior that people are responding to?" (*He or she who shames best has the most power.*)

DISCUSSION

1. Discuss the following questions from the "A Closer Look at God's Truth" section:

    - Read Proverbs 12:4. This verse makes a powerful statement about a wife's relationship with her husband. "Bones" in Scripture are analogous to strength. Another word for rottenness is decay. What is this verse telling us?

    - Read Genesis 2:23. This verse tells us that the woman is "bone of [her husband's] bone and flesh of [his] flesh." She is part of his own body. If a woman's behavior erodes and decays her husband's strength, what is she actually doing to herself?

    - If a man's behavior shames his wife, what would be the effect on him?

    - Shame weakens everybody—children, church family, community. Scripture tells us that believers are one Body. Ultimately, then, when we shame others, how does it affect us?

    - Read 2 Samuel 6:20-23. What price did Michal pay for her contemptuous behavior toward David?

    - The term for having no children is "barren." Think about this word in a spiritual sense. What does it mean to you?

ADDITIONAL DISCUSSION/ACTION STEPS

Go around the room and have the group members share the honest and truthful prayers they wrote to God for this chapter of the study (see page 49).

FIVE

CONTAGION OF SHAME (PART TWO)

Objective

To help group members learn how to personally break through their own shaming behavior and to encourage a long-term personal commitment to change their behavior patterns no matter what anyone else does.

Preparation

EXERCISE 1

Read and meditate on the following passage in Psalm 15:1-3, gathering your thoughts to share with the group:

> LORD, who may abide in Your tabernacle? Who may dwell in Your holy hill? He who walks uprightly, and works righteousness [acting and being right with God and others], and speaks the truth in his heart; He who does not backbite with his tongue, nor does evil to his neighbor, nor does he take up a reproach against his friend.

EXERCISE 2

Familiarize yourself with the diagram and explanation of the intimacy/shame cycles on page 95. This will be used during the Bible study. When discussing setting up an intimacy cycle, refer group members to this visual and commentary in their own books to help facilitate their understanding of the process.

DISCUSSION

Familiarize yourself with the discussion questions included in the following "Group Participation" section.

Group Participation

Exercise 1

Share the passage in Psalm 15:1-3 with the group and ask them to consider the following:

- It is very threatening to own—acknowledge and take responsibility for—who we really are, but it is essential to our healing and deliverance.

- This was a psalm of David who we know did not do everything right. He was, in fact, guilty of some very terrible behavior. Yet God said he was "a man after My own heart" (Acts 13:22). How was this so? Psalm 15:2 says that what God prizes is one who "speaks the truth in his heart"; one who, like David, will admit his or her wrong to God, to himself or herself, and to others.

- Outward behavior is never really the issue with God. It is only outward evidence of an inward problem. The real sin is always in the heart.

After sharing this Scripture and your thoughts concerning it with the group, ask for their responses to this question: "What is the inward sin that is indicated by outward shaming behavior toward others?" (*Self-protection, lack of trust in God, and so forth.*)

Exercise 2

Refer the group members to the following two pages in their books. Share the intimacy/shame cycles diagram with the group and then go through each of the points listed after the diagram. After you have done this with your group, discuss what kind of opting-out behaviors are the most instinctive to them.

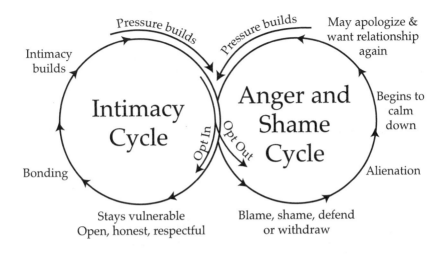

INTIMACY/SHAME CYCLES
WE'RE ALL GOING IN CIRCLES

1. Relationships can be said to be lived in a circular fashion. As the normal pressures of daily life (disagreements, disappointments, decision making) begin to build, they will need resolution in one form or another. We will either resolve them in the intimacy cycle or in the anger and shame cycle.

2. Notice that these two circles intersect. As the pressure builds, we will choose resolution by (1) being honest, open and perhaps even legitimately angry (but respectful and kind), and acknowledging our own feelings, thus staying in the intimacy cycle; or (2) resolving the pressure by opting out of the intimacy cycle and choosing to be controlled by our anger—blaming, shaming and punishing the other person.

3. Note that there is a moment of decision at which time we will choose which road to take.

4. Taking the first course, or "opting in" (choosing to remain vulnerable), will produce a safe environment for others in our life who may, for a time, continue to opt out. Eventually, if there is no one to join them in their anger and shaming, they often begin to see their own

behavior for what it is, start to take responsibility for it, and opt in for intimacy themselves.

5. There are many kinds of opting-out behaviors. Anger, rage, or verbal abuse are on one side, and on the other side are things such as the silent treatment, shaming thoughts, appeasement at the cost of truth, or simply avoiding the relationship.[1]

DISCUSSION

1. As time allows, discuss the following questions from the "A Closer Look at God's Truth" section:

    •   Read John 13:1-5. Jesus is washing the disciples' feet the night before His betrayal and crucifixion. What did Jesus know that enabled Him to humbly serve His disciples in this intimate way? Write down four things you discover from verse 3 that Jesus knew about Himself.

    •   Now read John 13:14-17. What do these verses tell us we are to do?

    •   If we are to do what He did, then we have to know what He knew. Can what was said about Him be said of us?

    •   How do John 14:2-3; 20:17; Galatians 4:4-7 and 1 John 4:4,6 refer to us? How do they correlate with what we have learned about Jesus in John 13?

2. Discuss the group's responses to the question in "A Closer Look at My Own Heart" (see page 55).

ADDITIONAL DISCUSSION/ACTION STEPS

Go around the room and have the group members share the prayer they paraphrased from Ephesians 1:15-23.

Note
1. Adapted from Kieth Robertson, IMET Seminar, "Anger/Intimacy."

CURE FOR SHAME (PART ONE)

Objective

To help group members personally identify the crippling lies that Satan uses to keep them from being their true selves before others.

Preparation

EXERCISE

On the top half of a whiteboard, flipchart or chalkboard, write the words "adversary," "opponent," "traducer," "defamer," "slanderer" and "accuser." Draw a line, and then below write the words "pure," "peaceable," "gentle," "reasonable," "merciful," "loving," "patient," "kind," "bearing all things," "believing all things," "hoping all things," "enduring all things."

DISCUSSION

Familiarize yourself with the discussion questions included in the following "Group Participation" section, or choose which questions you want to discuss with the group.

Group Participation

EXERCISE

Explain to the group that if we are going to be free from shame, we have to develop sharp discernment so that we immediately recognize whose voice we're hearing and, thus, "following" in our thought process. Refer the members to the words you wrote on the whiteboard, flipchart or chalkboard, and then discuss the following:

- Satan, or the devil, means adversary, opponent, traducer (causing humiliation or disgrace by making malicious and false statements), defamer, slanderer, accuser. With a name like that, what kind of messages do you think he would be communicating?

- How would the messages make you feel?

- What would his goal be?

Now state that on the other hand, James 3:17 tells us that God's wisdom—the wisdom that is from above—is first of all pure, then peaceable, gentle, reasonable, full of mercy and good fruits. First Corinthians 13:4,7 declares that love (which God is) is patient, kind, bears all things, believes all things, hopes all things, endures all things. (Refer the members to the second group of words on the whiteboard, chalkboard or flipchart as you discuss each of these terms.) Now ask the following:

- What kinds of messages would someone with these qualities communicate?

- How would these messages make you feel?

- What is God's goal?

Conclude the exercise by discussing how, then, we should discern which voice we are hearing.

DISCUSSION
1. Discuss the following questions from the "A Closer Look at God's Truth" section (or discuss the questions that you chose):

- Can you think of an area in your life that, while it may have a different expression than those areas of the people around you, may be a part of the whole? Briefly describe that area.

- Read 1 Corinthians 10:16-17. The communion of fellowship in the body and blood of Christ is a shared one—each person partakes from one loaf. How is the loaf made whole again? How does this truth apply to you?

- Read Romans 12:3-8. What gift do you think this woman might have? What gift doesn't she have?

- How does she illustrate the truth that what we sometimes interpret as unacceptable about ourselves is merely valid evidence of our limitation and is part of God's plan?

- Read Romans 15:4-7. How should knowing that we are a people in process, that we are not yet perfect and will not be in this lifetime, affect our attitude toward ourselves and others?

Additional Discussion/Action Steps

1. Discuss some of the responses that the participants listed in response to the question, "What is there about me that makes me unique?" on pages 64-65.

2. Talk about how God has created and gifted each of us to function in the place that He has prepared especially for us. What are some of the things God brought to their minds that they could be doing for someone else?

Cure for Shame
(Part Two)

Objective

To help group members identify that their susceptibility to shame is rooted in unbelief and mistrust of God.

Preparation

Familiarize yourself with the discussion questions included in the following "Group Participation" section, or choose which questions you want to discuss with the group.

Group Participation

1. Discuss the following questions from the "A Closer Look at God's Truth" section (or discuss the questions that you chose):

   • Read Exodus 33:12-13,18-23. When Moses became aware that God knew him by name, what request did he make of God (verses 13,18)? What was God's response?

   • Read Exodus 34:5-7. God Himself told Moses what He is really like. Correlate verse 7 with Exodus 20:5-6, which says God shows mercy to those who love Him and visits iniquity on those who hate Him. What do these verses tell us is the nature of God?

   • Moses' request to know God as intimately as he was known by God was the response of a maturing son. If God was pleased to respond to Moses' request to know Him, how do you think He would respond to yours?

- Read 1 John 4:8,16. Who do these verses tell you God is? Who is the object of His love?

- Read 2 Peter 1:2-3. From what do these verses tell us our peace will be derived?

- What "things" does 2 Peter 1:3 tell us God has provided for our life and godliness?

- Read Ephesians 1:3-6. According to these verses, when were we chosen?

- Why were we chosen? Give at least three reasons.

- Through whom does God achieve His purpose?

2. Discuss the following questions from the "A Closer Look at My Own Heart" section:

- Read Matthew 18:11-14 and ponder this thought: *If I had been the only person in the world who needed a redeemer, Jesus would have died for me.* What was it that moved Him to do this for you?

- How would you like this truth to transform your life?

ADDITIONAL DISCUSSION/ACTION STEPS

1. Ask members what would cause us to pretend we didn't see someone we knew or were acquainted with at the mall, grocery store or some other place.

2. Discuss what would prevent us from submitting a musical piece that we had written to a music director or an article that we had authored to a publisher.

3. Talk about some of the things the members might need to have in place before they (a) had company over, (b) went out, (c) spoke about something they didn't know well, or (d) spoke in front of a group.

4. Ask why these types of things tend to be important to us and what would happen if they were not in place. What would hinder us from really sharing our heart with someone?

5. Shame and fear of others go hand in hand. Psalm 56:11 says, "In God I have put my trust; I will not be afraid. What can man do to me?" Discuss what it says about our relationship with God if we are still fearing others' response to us.

EIGHT

CURE FOR SHAME (PART THREE)

Objective

To help group members gain a personal revelation of the love of the Father for them and His desire to be known by them and to have an intimate relationship with them.

Preparation

Familiarize yourself with the discussion questions included in the following "Group Participation" section, or choose which questions you want to discuss with the group. For this study, you will also want to be sure to discuss the items listed in the additional discussion questions section. Note that while some of the answers in this section are offered, you should be prepared with your own contributions as well. Allow group members to share first, but be sure to emphasize the answers that articulate our theme. Also note that for the sake of clarity the questions are addressed to those with children, but be careful to include in the discussion those who don't. Even if some do not have children, everyone is somebody's child and can imagine the right answers.

Group Participation

1. Discuss the following questions from the "A Closer Look at God's Truth" section (or discuss the questions that you chose):

    · Read Ephesians 2:18. What does this verse say about us?

    · Through whom do we have access?

- Read Genesis 1:26-27 and Romans 8:28-29. What do these verses tell us God is doing in us?

- Read Ephesians 3:14-21. From whom does the whole family in heaven and earth derive its name (nature, character)?

- What do the terms "rooted" and "grounded" mean to you?

- What is the result of being rooted and grounded in Christ's love?

ADDITIONAL DISCUSSION/ACTION STEPS

1. Explain how the bottom line of shame is fear of rejection and abandonment—a fear that we would find ourselves isolated and alone in this world. Our Father God has placed us in families, and He has done this to:

   - Make sure we have a place where we feel we belong, a place to love and be loved, a place where we would get our name and identity.

   - Reveal the nature of His own heart toward us. Even though families are imperfect (and some more than others), they still represent something God wants us to know about Himself.

2. Answer and discuss the following questions:

   - For those of you who have children, did you decide to have them because they already loved you? (*No, it was an extension of the love of the parents. They wanted offspring on which they could shower their love.*)

   - Is there anything your children could ever do that would destroy your love for them? (*For most, the answer would be no, especially for women. As parents we might be sad, grieved and maybe even angry about our children's choices, but we would still love them.*)

   - How far would you go to protect the welfare of your children? (*Most parents would give their lives for them if need be.*)

- When your children become mature, what is the one thing concerning your relationship that you hope will continue? (*That it would be more reciprocal—that the children would want to know the parents as adults; that they would call, visit, share their lives with their parents and, hopefully, express their love to them.*)

- Each of us were created in God's image. Because of this, where do you think your passion for your children originated? (*From our Father God!*)

- God's fundamental identity is as a father. All that God has done in creation has issued forth from His Father's heart. The nature of His fatherhood is what He wants us to know most about Him. To achieve wholeness, to become free from ourselves and our self-protective strategies, it is essential that we come to know Him in this most wonderful aspect of His nature. What do your desires for your children tell you about the Father's heart?

What Is Aglow International?

From one nation to 172 worldwide...
From one fellowship to more than 4,600...
From 100 people to more than 17 million...

Aglow International has experienced phenomenal growth since
its inception 40 years ago. In 1967, four women from the state
of Washington prayed for a way to reach out to other Christian
women in simple fellowship, free from denominational boundaries.

The first meeting held in Seattle, Washington, USA, drew more
than 100 women to a local hotel. From that modest beginning,
Aglow International has become one of the largest intercultural,
interdenominational women's organizations in the world.

Each year, an estimated 17 million people are ministered to
through Aglow's local fellowship meetings, Bible studies, support
groups, retreats, conferences and various outreaches. From the
inner city to the upper echelons, from the woman next door to
the corporate executive, Aglow seeks to minister to the felt
needs of women around the world.

Christian women find Aglow a "safe place" to grow spiritually
and begin to discover and use the gifts, talents and abilities God
has given them. Aglow offers excellent leadership training and
varied opportunities to develop those leadership skills.

Undergirding the evangelistic thrust of the ministry is an empha-
sis on prayer, which has led to an active prayer network linking
six continents. The vast prayer power available through Aglow
women around the world is being used by God to influence
countless lives in families, communities, cities and nations.

Aglow's Mission Statement

Our mission is to lead women to Jesus Christ and provide opportunity for Christian women to grow in their faith and minister to others.

—◦◦◦—

Aglow's Continuing Focus...

- To reconcile a woman to her womanhood as God designed. To strengthen and empower her to fulfill the unfolding plan of God as He brings restoration to the male/female relationship, which is the foundation of the home, the church and the community.
- To love women of all cultures, with a special focus on Muslim women.
- To reach out to every strata of society, from inner cities to isolated outposts to our own neighborhoods, with very practical and tangible expressions of the love of Jesus.

—◦◦◦—

Aglow Ministers In...

Albania, Angola, Anguilla, Antigua, Argentina, Aruba, Australia, Austria, Bahamas, Bahrain, Barbados, Belarus, Belgium, Belize, Benin, Bermuda, Bolivia, Botswana, Brazil, Britain, Bulgaria, Burkina Faso, Cameroon, Canada, Chile, China, Colombia, Congo (Dem. Rep. of), Congo (Rep. of), Costa Rica, Côte d'Ivoire, Cuba, Curaçao, Czech Republic, Denmark, Djibouti, Dominica, Dominican Republic, Ecuador, Egypt, El Salvador, Equatorial Guinea, Estonia, Ethiopia, Faroe Islands, Fiji, Finland, France, Gabon, the Gambia, Germany, Ghana, Grand Cayman, Greece, Grenada, Guam, Guatemala, Guinea, Guyana, Haiti, Honduras, Hungary, Iceland, India, Indonesia, Ireland, Israel, Jamaica, Japan, Kazakstan, Kenya, Korea, Kyrgyzstan, Latvia, Lithuania, Malawi, Malaysia, Mali, Mauritius, Mexico, Mongolia, Mozambique, Myanmar, Nepal, Netherlands, New Zealand, Nicaragua, Niger, Nigeria, Norway, Oman, Pakistan, Panama, Papua New Guinea, Peru, Philippines, Portugal, Puerto Rico, Romania, Russia, Rwanda, Samoa, Samoa (American), Scotland, Senegal, Serbia, Sierra Leone, Singapore, South Africa, Spain, Sri Lanka, St. Kitts, St. Lucia, St. Maartan, St. Vincent, Sudan, Suriname, Sweden, Switzerland, Tajikistan, Tanzania, Thailand, Togo, Tonga, Trinidad/Tobago, Turks & Caicos Islands, Uganda, Ukraine, United States, Uruguay, Uzbekistan, Venezuela, Vietnam, Virgin Islands (American), Virgin Islands (British), Wales, Yugoslavia, Zambia, Zimbabwe, and other nations.

How do I find my nearest Aglow Fellowship? Call or write us at:

AGLOW
INTERNATIONAL

P.O. Box 1749, Edmonds, WA 98020-1749
Phone: 425-775-7282 or 1-800-793-8126
Fax: 425-778-9615   E-mail: aglow@aglow.org
Web site: http://www.aglow.org/

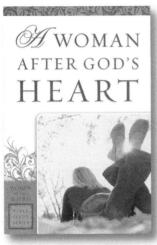
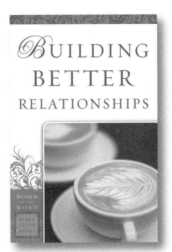

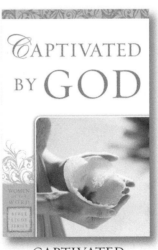